How Canadians Can Get Out Of

DEBT

and Save

MONEY

CHRISTINE VICTORIA

authorHOUSE®

AuthorHouse™
1663 Liberty Drive
Bloomington, IN 47403
www.authorhouse.com
Phone: 1 (800) 839-8640

Published by AuthorHouse   06/23/2016

ISBN: 978-1-5246-1569-7 (sc)
ISBN: 978-1-5246-1568-0 (e)

Print information available on the last page.

This book is printed on acid-free paper.

CONTENTS

INTRODUCTION

Random people are knocking at your door. The bills keep piling up. Letters keep filling your mail box. You have creditors calling you at work and you don't know what to do. It all seems so overwhelming and the idea of being debt-free seems like a distant dream. I am here to tell you it is not. I owed well over my credit limit. This debt grew since I came out of school and increased with consumer debt from mindless spending. I then said enough was enough and decided this was no way to live. You too can feel the bliss of not owing but actually saving. What is better than having money in the bank and being able to reach your financial goals and dreams?

The primary audience for this book are people who are in debt. This can be students with education loans, adults with mortgages or senior citizens wanting to retire but not knowing how. It is also a great guide to those who just want to learn more about their finances and find ways to save or make more money. Whatever your endeavor, this book is the answer.

You will learn to analyze your spending and effectively budget. You will shift from owing to being a saver. You will learn new ways of generating income and find out how you can grow your money. I guide you step by step on how you can improve your financial situation. In addition to supplying you with practical tools and tips. I have added informative questionnaires that will help you learn more about yourself. I will teach you by giving you weekly goal objectives that will help you to get closer to your dreams.

I have simplified your goal of being debt free and have broken it down into 8 simple steps.

Step 1 (week 1 & 2): Calculate how much debt you have

Step 2 (week 3): Add up all your expenses

Step 3 (week 4): Find out how much you make

Step 4 (week 5 & 6): Make a budget and learn how to use a spending journal

Step 5 (week 7): Generate more money to pay debt off faster

Step 6 (week 8 & 9): You need to cut your expenses

Step 7 (week 10): Pay yourself first

Step 8 (week 11 & 12): Grow your savings

Just 8 steps and in 3 months you will be on your way to a better financial future. What I did took effort and my result was based on my commitment to my goal. Supplemental materials you will need are a notebook or binder with lined loose leaf pages. Pen, whiteout, pencil and highlighters are also good utensils. You will need them to make notes and to complete weekly objectives. If you are committed and are willing to put in the work then, read on.

Step 1 (week 1 & 2): Calculate how much debt you have

This is the first thing that I did. I faced up to my debt and added up how much I owed and using the interest calculated how much I was really paying my creditors.

CHAPTER 1

Assessing the Situation

How much do you owe?

This is the hardest part. Instead of shoving bills into a drawer and ignoring phone calls from collection agencies, you have to face your problem. You have to know how much debt you are in, in order to get out of it. Week 1 and 2 will be devoted to collecting all your statements and adding up how much you owe. My recommendation is get a binder or notebook to write in. This will help you to organize your bills and calculate the amount of debt you have. I went through my bills and highlighted important numbers like the amount of interest I was paying, due dates and the total debt I had to pay. I would circle parts of the bill I didn't understand and called the representative who explained my bill. If you see any charges that were added to any of your bills that you are sure you did not incur then bring it to the representative attention. You can always dispute a bill. Once you have tallied all the numbers write them down in list format. Number each creditor and indicate the total amount you owe, then beside it write the interest. Beside that write the minimum or monthly payment. You can make a simple chart like below which will help you to see how much money you are actually paying.

Example:

Creditor	debt	interest	minimum payment
Credit card visa	$800	19%	$162
Line of credit	$1500	5%	$85
Mortgage	$15,000	4.5%	$700

This helped me to see how much money I was actually paying compared to what I thought I owed.

Transfer, Consolidate or Negotiate

You can see how quickly debt can accumulate. Some debt is good debt like having a mortgage. You might owe more but you are actually building an investment because your goal is to own your property. Bad debt is consumer debt as seen here with the credit card and lines of credit.

A mortgage can be seen as a fixed expense depending on if you have a fixed mortgage versus an open one. If you have an open mortgage then you can take advantage if there are lower interest rates. But if the rates are higher then you are better off with a fixed mortgage because you will be locked in at a specific rate which means it won't go up but you also have to be aware it won't go down either if rates are lower. You will be able to make an extra payment towards your principal but simply accelerating your mortgage. This means that if you can afford to pay only 1134.56 per month then you would break the payment in half to two $523.65 payments. Every payment will be made biweekly instead of monthly. This extra payment could save a year off your mortgage. If you have a 25 year mortgage at 300,000 with a 20% down payment then you will cut it down to 24 years. If you break down your payment further and pay $283.64 weekly you will end up saving 3 years off your mortgage and saving you $15, 877 in interest. You can also save by changing the amortization down to 15 years. You will save you 40,000 of amortization costs. Many financial institutions have mortgage calculators just go online and plug in your information and change the frequency of payment as well as the amortization. See what you can afford and the ways you could save. You could also book an appointment with your mortgage specialist to discuss different rates and ask questions.

With your credit card debt and line of credit, if you just paid the minimum payment it would take you several months or years to get out of debt. Let's calculate. Take the amount you owe and times it by the interest and itself. For example credit card $800 x 119% = $952. This means you are actually paying $952. This is $152 more. Now Take $952 and divide it by the minimum payment. $952 ÷ 162 = 5.8

This means it will take you 5 close to 6 months to get out of debt. You should always pay more than the minimum payment. I calculated how many months it would take to pay off my debt. I cut this amount in half by increasing the amount I could afford to pay. I did this by simply following my eight steps. I looked where I was spending money and cut back as wells as looked for areas I could save. I also paid my highest debt first and then worked on my other debt.

Creditor	debt	minimum payment	total payout	months
Visa	$800	$162	$952	5.8
Line of credit	$1500	$85	$1575	18.5
Mortgage	$15000	$700	$15675	22.3

Total debt: $17300 Total debt with interest: paying: $18202

Focus your attention on the debt that has the highest interest. You should try to pay it off first. If you need to pay as much as you can to the highest interest creditor and the minimum payments for the rest. Once you have that creditor paid off then you continue to the next highest interest and repeat the process until you are out of debt.

Another option that you have is to negotiate with the creditor to lower your interest rate. This will reduce your debt greatly and enable you to make more payments toward the debt. In this situation with the credit card being so high in interest I would use my line of credit to pay the whole credit card bill off so I would just deal with a 5 % interest instead of a 19%. The line of credit you will owe $2300 at 5% interest which means you are actually paying $2415 instead of $2527. This is a savings of $112.

If it all gets confusing and seems overwhelming. You can call a debt counselling service which will assist you with your debts. They assist you with budgeting and help you avoid bankruptcy. If you just can keep up with the payments an option is to consolidate. This mean the Credit Counselling Company will negotiate with your creditors and take all of your debt and lump it into one lower payment a month. This is a more difficult approach due to the fact that you might need to get someone to cosign the agreement for you. If you really feel that debt is too much then bankruptcy is the last and final option. I don't recommend unless you are desperate. Being bankrupt means you have a zero credit score and will affect you being able to buy a house or get a car.

Credit Score Report

There are many companies out there that will help you obtain a credit report. This gives you a score telling you how good you are to creditors as a borrower. This number is what companies look at and help them to decide whether they should give you a loan or not. Equifax and TransUnion are free. You have two options. You can either print out and fill an application and send it by mail. Another option is to get your report electronically. Keep your report in your financial binder. You should obtain a copy of your credit score every year. This ensures that you know where you stand. You can speak with a representative and they can explain further about what your score means and how you can improve it. You might be worried because every time someone looks into your credit it shows as a hit on your report. There are soft hit and hard hits. You looking to your score means that you have a soft hit which won't affect your score as much.

Some ways of improving your score include:

- Know your score
- Paying your bills in full each month or more than the minimum payment.
- Don't go over your credit limit.
- Pay your bills on time. Make note on a calendar when your bills are due. If for some reason the date is not good for you then you could call your creditor up and ask them to move it to a different date that is closer to when you get paid.
- Don't close unused credit card accounts. Keeping cards that have no fee open allows you to have more credit available to you. The more credit you have available to you the higher your score.

What I did to get out of debt and save my credit score was lock my credit card in a box to stop me from using it. I paid as much as I could towards the debt so more than the minimum payment. Once my debt was paid off I began to use my credit card again. This time I would write down my purchases and pay off my credit card bill in full each month.

By the end of the first two weeks you should have added up all your debt. You should have organized and managed your debt by transferring, negotiating or consolidating. You also have obtained your credit report. By reading it and making plans to improve your score you are now on your way to a better financial future.

Step 2 (week 3): Add up all your expenses

By Adding up all my expenses I was able to see where my money was going. This helped me to realize all my costs and see how much I was spending.

CHAPTER 2

Spending Analysis

What Type of Spender are you?

1) When grocery shopping you . . .
   a) Grab whatever looks good
   b) Get chips and chocolate you need something to comfort you since you've had a hard week.
   c) Look at what's marked down
   d) Shop at the more expensive store
   e) Shop with a list

2) Your dream vacation would be . . .
   a) Los Vegas Casino You need a little fun
   b) Cruise ship because you feel like it
   c) Cuba because it's affordable
   d) Spa resort in California
   e) Staycation I have to spring clean my house

3) What type of mall do you shop at?
   a) Dollar store
   b) Where ever I feel like shopping
   c) Anywhere there's a deal
   d) High class boutique
   e) Forget the mall you have enough stuff

4) My ideal house would be . . .
   a) Condo
   b) Cozy Cabin
   c) Bungalow
   d) Mansion
   e) Apartment

5) When you look at the receipt after a shopping trip you . . .
   a) Wonder how I overspent when I only purchased little things
   b) Sometimes go over or under budget depending on my mood
   c) Are shocked at the amount considering you bought only sale items
   d) I don't look at the receipt. I but things because I deserve them.
   e) On budget I but what I need

Mostly A-Mindless Spender

You spend money without thinking. This may be because you are lazy or you just don't realize where your money is going. It's all about convenience items like bottled water, prepackaged store bought food and Tim Horton's coffee. Your coffee habit end up costing you more in the long run. If you spend $3-$4 every day on coffee you will be spending $90 to $120 per month which means about $1000 per year. You should make your coffee at home during the weekdays and treat yourself to a store bought cup on the weekends this will end up saving you money and closer to being debt free. I was a mindless spender ordering takeout instead of picking up my order or grocery shopping and preparing meals at home. I found taxes and delivery fees added up doubling the cost of my order. When you were just craving a slice of pizza where if you bought it and picked it up from the store would only cost you about $5. But since you are too lazy to pick it up then you would order it. Some places may even have a minimum delivery requirement such as your order must be $25 or more in order for them to deliver to you. They will add an extra $6 for delivery, $3 to tip the driver and taxes. That pizza craving would cost you about $40 and now you have the rest of the pizza you don't know what to do with since you'll only eat one or two slices.

Mostly B-Emotional Spender

If you're having a bad day a trip to the mall is just what you need for a pick me up. You spend when you are sad, happy or mad. Whatever your feeling you bought an outfit for it. You are an emotional spender. My advice is keep your credit card locked up and when using your debit card first ask yourself do you really need this item. How is your mood? How do you feel? You shouldn't be shopping to make yourself feel better. You should buy stuff only when you need it. You might need to see a counsellor or therapist to help you with your feelings. I used to do this and in fact we are all guilty of it. I would buy purses just to make me happy if I had a hard day. Instead now I evaluate my wardrobe every month and if I need something like a pair of shorts I will write it down on a piece of paper. I will keep an eye out for sales on summer clothes and buy my shorts marked down. Not only do I buy something I need but I also save money too.

Mostly C-Sale Spender

If it's on sale you have to have it even if you don't have a use for it. You get a high every time you save money. But are you really saving money? If you have 12 sweaters a home and you are buying another one for $30 or 50% off then you are not saving money. You are spending money you didn't need to spend. You should make a list of things you need then assign an amount you can afford to spend on that item. Then you can look at sales to buy the items you need. Ask the sales clerk and mark down on a calendar when the sales for specific seasonal items occur.

Mostly D-Entitled Spender

You feel you deserve the finer things in life but don't realize your lifestyle is what is causing you to be in debt. Its fine to treat yourself once in a while but spending on luxuries every day is effecting your wallet. May be you are just used to the lifestyle your parents brought you up in and you grew up in a rich home. Or maybe your parents were poor and you are overcompensating for what you didn't get when you were little. Either way you need to recognize you have a problem and you need to question whether you are buying an item for necessity or luxury. What I do to see whether or not I should buy something is to write down what it is I want to buy and calculate the hours of work it would take to afford that item. For example a manicure can cost around $40. If you only make minimum wage which is $11.25 you would need to work three and a half hours.

Ex. $40 \div $11.25 = 3.55

Is it really worth the hard three and a half hours you put into work? If you really want the service then find out another way you can get it. One option is to give yourself a manicure you can get $10 nail polish that is marked down to $3 if you wait for sales and know where to look. If you miss the professional touch why not call up local beauty schools. They will tell you when their students are doing lessons on things like hair, make up, and massages. They will likely need someone to practice on. Some colleges offer their students services for free or at a discount. You could be saving yourself lots of money and helping someone out as well.

Mostly E-Need Spender

You only buy what you need which is great because you recognize the value of money. The issue is you don't treat yourself to anything. You deserve a vacation and to eat out once in a while. If you are in debt it simply is because you aren't making enough money and should consider cutting your expenses or getting a second job.

Expenses

Now that you have taken the quiz it will help you see where your money is going. Write down in your notebook what your result was. Are you a sale spender or an emotional spender? Write down the reasons why you got this result. Jot down how you plan on correcting this behavior. It will help you to analyze your spending. This is where the hard part comes in. Take 3 to 6 months' worth of statements for your bank account and credit statement. Write your expenses in different categories. Divide your expenses into two sections one is for fixed expenses and the other for variable. This will help you see what expenses you have and whether or not you can lower the amount of money you spend in each category. Take a look at where your money is going. Are you eating out a lot? You may need to think about how your take out habit is effecting your wallet.

Fixed Expenses

The word fixed mean that these are the types of expenses that don't change from month to month. Like your mortgage, car payment, insurance for your house and house taxes. It's important to know how much you spend and which date of the month these payment go out of your bank account. Mark the dates on a calendar. This ensures you have enough money in the bank to cover these expenses and won't go into overdraft.

Variable Expenses

Variable means that it changes every month. This means entertainment, clothing, groceries, and eating take out. You don't always need to buy clothes every month and the amount of money you spend for your clothes varies. Add up the amount of money you spent per category and average the money out to equal one month of spending. For example for entertainment for 6 months I spent $800 then divide it by 6 you get $133 per month. Don't throw away receipts. You should make a habit of keeping your receipts and recording how much you spent on what to see where your money goes.

Now you have identified your spending mistakes and seen where your money is going. You have learned the difference between fixed and variable expenses as well as recorded the cost of each expense. Now on to the next step.

Step 3 (week 4): Find out how much you make

I was surprised by how much money I had coming in and how much of it I was wasting because I viewed it as petty cash. I was able to boost my income 5%.

CHAPTER 3

Income

You might be surprised how much money you get. Everyone just thinks of their weekly pay check and never considers extra money that they get like bonuses. By looking at your income you can see whether you generate enough money per month or if you should consider putting serious effort into finding ways you can make more money.

Wage/salary

This is how much you make at your job. In order to find this amount you can look at your pay stubs and add them up per month or look at your income tax form and average the cost per month. Your money might vary say if you work in retail and your hours change each week depending on the season. You might get more hours at Christmas and less in January when the season is over. You might have two jobs and therefore have to record your two incomes. Either way find out on average how much you make per month. Take the net pay into account not your gross earnings. The government deducts a lot of taxes and you might think you are making $50,000 a year when you actually netting $37,000.

Gifts

Don't forget the extra money you get from your relatives at birthdays or Christmas. This money is money that you use. Other gifts might be tips that you make if you are a bartender or server. Instead of spending your tips mindlessly you should collect them in a jar and at the end of the month see how much you make. Your yearly Christmas bonus should be averaged out to add to your monthly income. I added about 5% to my income with gift money. This was money I used to spend foolishly and was unaccounted.

Freelance/Hobbies

Another way you generate income is with the extra work you do. You might clean houses on the weekend for cash. Maybe you are a freelance writer for online magazines or maybe you have a hobby that makes you money like making crafts for a Christmas bazaar. You might even make money off a garage sale you had in the summer or you sold some stuff online.

Refunds and Rebates

Many companies offer rebates on electronics such as televisions or lap tops. You can find them on their company website. You can print it out fill it and send it to get money back from your purchase. This can be as much as $100. Will that money you shouldn't just spend it. You should either use it to pay off a bill and become closer to being debt free or put it into savings.

Money is everywhere you just have to look deeper to identify what your sources of income are. By adding up the money you make you can truly see which sources you take for granted. By seeing the value of each source you now realize the actual amount of income you earn. You are less likely to see tips as just pocket change when you pool your tips into a jar at the end of the month and count it. Instead of wasting that money by spending it items such as magazines or make up which don't last long. You can save it for a few months and use it to buy a larger, and longer lasting purchase such as a car. It will serve your needs better and will transport you to and from work which then is a tool that contributes to your ability to earn an income.

Step 4 (week 5-6): Make a budget and learn to use a spending journal

CHAPTER 4

Monthly Budget

Monthly Budget	
Income	
Wage	
Bonus/Tips	
Gifts	
Refunds	
Total Income	

Expenses	
Fixed Expenses	

Home	Insurance
Mortgage/Rent	Home
Electricity	Auto
Gas	Medical
Water	Disability
Phone	
Cell Phone	
Cable	**Other**
Internet	Car payment
Property Taxes	Gym membership
Child care	

Total Fixed Expenses

Variable Expenses	
Living	**Medical**
Groceries	Medications
Personal	Eye Glasses
Clothing	Dentist
Education	
Eating Out	
Salon	
Pets	
Entertainment	
Transportation (gas)	
Other	
Total Variable Expenses	
Total Expenses	
Total Income minus Total Expenses	

By budgeting I was able to plan how much money I was spending and where. This allowed me to take control of my money.

Week 5 to 6 is all about budgeting. So you will have to make time in your busy schedule to follow these steps and make a proper budget. You can use excel or if you aren't into technology then you can just create a budget in your notebook. Make sure to include your different areas of income and total them under each category. See the sample budget. Now divide your expenses into categories. Here what is used is home expenses, insurance and other for fixed expenses and living expenses and medical expenses are used for variable expenses. This is what I use.

Fixed Expenses

Fixed expenses are payments you make monthly that stay the same as explained in chapter 2. I have divided this category into three sub categories that are seen as a requirement. We all need shelter and have costs associated with keeping our homes warm and suppling it with heat and electricity. We also need to insure our homes in the case of fire or flooding. And we all have other fixed expenses such as car payments to make.

Home Expense

I have used this category heading in order to organize everything to do with owning a home or renting. Things like mortgage, rent, taxes, electricity, gas, and water. These are what keep your house up in running. Again it is merely a suggestive heading. You can divide your expenses anyway you feel like it. Fixed expenses that are associated with the home which are luxuries are home phone, cell phone, cable and internet. These are things you can cut back on that are nice to have but are not necessary.

Insurance

Having insurance is very important. If you own a home you want to make sure that if a fire or flood happens you have the money to fix it up. Another important type of insurance is title insurance. With all the fraud that happens now a days we need to make sure that if someone sells our house without our permission we will get our money back. If renting you need renter's insurance. This is just like for the home it protects you against environmental emergencies such as fire and if you have valuables stolen you are protected. You would have to find a reputable insurance company and go over their agreement before you sign to make sure all your need are met and that you are protected for all things that could happen to your home.

Other

I have added an open sub category to show you that not everything that is an expense can be lumped into a category.

This is okay because you now have the opportunity to include a variety of expenses in your budget. One example is if you are financing or leasing a vehicle and another would be a gym member ship such as seen in this budget.

Variable Expenses

These are expenses which vary from month to month. Medical expenses are included because you will need to pay for things like medication and other health care needs. You might not have benefits at work and will need to pay out of pocket. I have also included a sub category titled Living Expenses and this has to do with the daily activities you participate in.

Medical Expense

This involves doctors' bills, prescription fees, glasses, and dental work. This is if you don't have benefits at work and need to pay out of pocket.. Maybe you like to get massages or need to see a nutritionist or naturopath. This is where you can organize that expense.

Living Expenses

It is anything that involves your daily activities. This means activities like eating, shopping for clothes or even transportation to and from work. You can expand this category and include your transportation such as gas for your car. How you set up your budget is your choice.

Now that you have set up your sections you will then need to use some math to calculate all the money you spend each month. Here is a step by step process.

Step 1 – First fill out your income.

Step 2 - Next fill out your fixed expenses.

Step 3 - Enter the amount of money per month you are using to pay off your debt.

Step 4 – For your variable expenses assign a number to each expense that you can afford to pay.

Step 5 - Add every category up.

Step 6 – Take your income and subtract your expenses.

If you still have money left over then you did a good job. If you are left with no money or you are owing then you have to go back to your variable expenses and give them a lower number. How you should divide your expenses should be around 30% of your income for housing, 10% for debt repayment, 5% savings, 25% transportation, 25% living expenses, 2.5% medical, and 2.5% for other. Once your debt is paid off you can then put that money towards savings so you would then aim for 15 %.

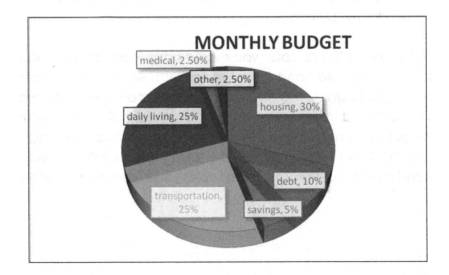

If you couldn't possibly go any lower then maybe you need to find way you can save more money or you need to generate more income.

Spending Journal

This is an important tool that you should use to keep track of where your money is going. Go to your local dollar store and buy a small pocket sized note book. Every time you go to the bank or do online banking you should record your bank account balance. When you go out and spend money for things like groceries. You should record where and what you spent your money on. Then you take your balance and subtract the amount you spent. You can ask the cashier or simply look at your receipt. You are them left with the amount of money you have left in your account. This allows you to always know how much is in your account as well as lets you keep track of where your money is going. You will avoid going in overdraft by using this technique. This technique is what saved me. I used to be embarrassed when my debit was declined at a store and would use my credit card as back up. Now I avoid using my credit card as back up and simply look at how much I have in the bank and judge if it is enough for my purchase.

By the end of this chapter you should have learned about the different expenses and how to identify them when you are creating a budget. You also effectively learned how to create a budget and use a spending journal. You should review your budget every month and use your spending journal every day. By doing these two things you are taking responsibility for your spending and controlling it. This enables you to save more money.

Step 5 (week 7): Generate More Money to pay debt off faster

Each month I would make it my goal to find a new way I could generate more income. By doing so I was able to use that extra income to pay my debt off faster.

CHAPTER 5

Extra Income

Some people might find that their money is just not enough compared to the amount of bills that are piling up. One solution is to generate more income. This is the moment where you can get creative and think of ways that you can get more money. Once your bills are paid off the best part is that you will have extra money to put towards your savings.

Work

If you are happy with your job then the simple solution is to either pick up more shifts at work or get up the courage to ask your boss for a raise. If you are currently working full time then the second option is that you can get a part time job on the side on the weekends or in the evenings. If you aren't making enough and you think there are other jobs out there that pay more that you are better suited for then the third option is to spread your wings and you can find another job that not only better uses your skills and abilities but also pays more.

Declutter

If you have a lot of stuff that you don't need then selling your items maybe just what you need for extra cash. You can have a garage sale or sell your items online. There are many websites that let you sell your stuff for free or at a low cost. Sites like Amazon, kijiji, and craigslist. Your apartment will feel lighter with less stuff while your wallet will get heavier.

Get Creative

If you are really good with your hands then you can make stuff that people want to buy like crafts such as wood carvings, or knitted scarfs. These are items that you can sell online on etsy or ebay. If the internet isn't your thing then think about renting a table at a local church bazaar or craft show. I know around Christmas time people are looking for gifts and they especially love meaningful homemade items to give to their family.

Showcase your cooking abilities

If you like to bake or cook you can sell your creations at a bake sale. Another option is if you are really talented and have education in cooking you can teach classes at your grocery store. Longos and fortinos both offer classes.

Drive your way to more money

Do you enjoy driving? Know your way around your city? Have a comfortably seated car that's great on gas? You can make money by driving people around. Websites like Uber are good to use for extra cash.

Sports

Enjoy sports and do you have good teaching skills? Maybe you should consider getting a job as a soccer or hockey coach for kid's teams. If you are good with kids then maybe you could offer your services as a baby sitter as well.

Pets

Do you love animals? Get a job at your local pet store as an animal care attendant. You could also open your own business and walk dogs or pet sit for your neighbors.

Landscaping services

Everybody loves to see the seasons change snow falling in winter, flowers growing in spring and leaves changing in the fall. No one wants the extra work yard work to shovel snow, cut grass, or rake leaves. You can provide these services to your neighborhood. You can put adds up at the senior center and market your services specifically for seniors. If you have a green thumb you could expand your services to planting gardens and trimming trees.

Clean, Clean, Clean

Another job that no one wants to do is clean their house. You can offer house cleaning at a discount compared to companies in your area.

Tutor

Were you good at school when you were younger? If you are up to date with current information and have excellent skills you can tutor courses at your local college. You might just have to speak with the professor and purchase a used textbook for a low fee to familiarize yourself with the course.

Write

If you think you have what it takes to be a writer then you can freelance for companies like about.com or start your own blog.

Temping

Maybe temping is an option for you. You can go online and submit your application to various temp agencies in your area. The jobs vary from factory work to telemarketing.

Rent out

If you have extra space in your house or an empty furnished basement. Think about renting a room or apartment as added income. You should get a lawyer to write up a rental contract. This insures that you are protected against bad tenants.

Recycle

After a party has gone on at your neighbor's house you can offer to take their empty alcohol bottles to the liquor store for cash. You could even go around your city on recycling day and look through bins for empties. There is a lady on my street that I see Monday mornings going around on her bicycle collecting bottles. It seems like mere pocket change but it can added up to great savings. If you only get $5 per week you would make $260 a year. If you put it into savings you could get $1000 in 5 years. That could be used to purchase a new laptop or as a mortgage payment.

Get paid for shopping

Plan to shop online. A great site is ebates. They give you a certain percentage of your money back when you shop. This would be an ideal site for those of you who are personal shoppers. If you shop a lot you will find that you can get a lot of money.

As you can see the avenues you can take to increase your cash flow are endless. Take your notebook and jot down five more extra jobs that you could do that aren't on this list. Think about it. Now pick one or two and make a plan on how you can start providing your services to begin earning money and paying off your debt sooner.

Step 6 (week 8 &9): You need to cut your expenses

Cutting my expenses took a bit more work since it meant more shopping around and negotiating for cheaper prices. I was able to cut my expenses by 42.5%. This meant I could use my money and put it towards paying off my creditors and into my savings account.

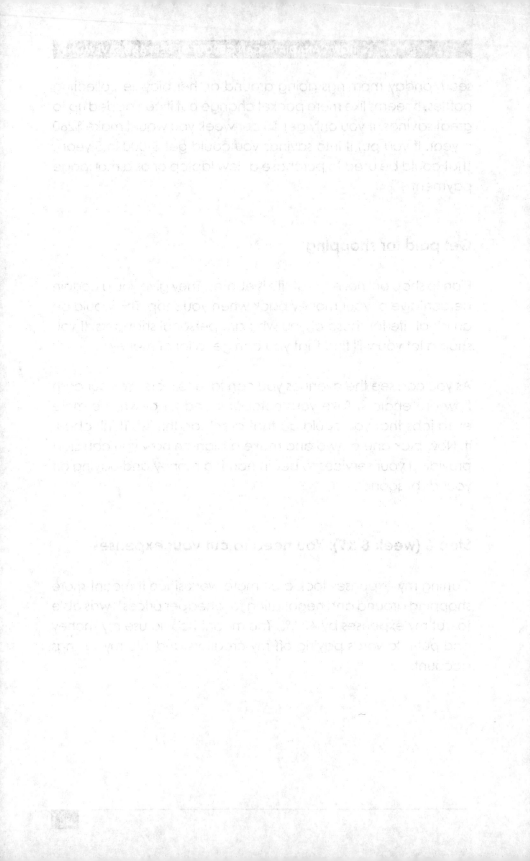

CHAPTER 6

How to save money

The two ways of getting in the black are by making more money or cutting back. Chapter 5 showed you ways of making more money. Now you need to reexamine what you are spending your money on and whether or not you can save more money.

Housing Expenses

Can't keep up with your mortgage payment? Maybe the type of house you choose is too expensive for your current age or lifestyle. If you are a senior a house is simply too big for your to clean and keep up with the maintenance. Your children have left the nest so it's time for you to get a smaller one. If you live in a two-story house consider a cheaper bungalow. One floor is easier for senior living and the lower floor can be rented out for extra income. Maybe instead of all the cost associated with owning a home renting would be cheaper for you. You can go to an apartment where hydro is included. You won't have to pay property taxes any more. Or if you live on your own consider moving into an apartment with a roommate where you can split expenses. I personally live in shared accommodations. Some people view it as being to frugal and they couldn't live with other people but I see it as a way of socializing and added money I can put into my retirement. By living with other people I cut my rent in half. This cuts my house expense from 30% to 25 % of my budget. I saved 5%.

Phone/Cell Phone/Cable/Internet

Do you really need all those channels? Maybe you should go for a cheaper cable package or phone plan. There are many companies offering deals and discounts. You can switch providers or negotiate with your current provider to lower your bill. Since cable providers don't want their customers to leave some will add free channels to your subscription. Instead of having two phones you should ditch your home phone and just use your cell phone. To save minutes on your cell phone you should use email instead of texting or calling. Instead of having a monthly phone bill I use a pay and talk card. I cut 10% of my budget using pay and talk and limiting my conversations.

Bank accounts

With all the different types of banks that we have today. You have the opportunity to go online and research which bank can provide you with cheaper and better services. Look for a bank that has a checking account with no fee or a low fee that you can afford. Shop around for deals. If you are a student some banks offer you a discounted monthly service fee. See how many transactions they give you per month and consider how many you would need. Don't bounce checks or go into overdraft. You will be adding unnecessary charges. To avoid ATM fees, when I need cash I use the cash back option when making a purchase in store. Determine how much money you need ahead of time and make less withdraws to avoid transaction fees. I found I was happy with my services and I didn't use cash to often so I was on budget with this category.

Food

Eat out less. You should make and bring your lunch and coffee to work each morning. By making your meals at home you are saving thousands of dollars each year. I used to eat out a lot and buying lunch everyday cost me around $10 per meal or $50 per week. For one year I spent $2600 on just eating out. Since then I started grocery shopping and I look at my newspaper and look for sales on food. You can save by only making meals with items that were on sale that week. Look for cheap meal ideas online. You can also use coupons. Sites like gocoupons, save.ca or brandsaver give you the option of printing coupons at home or mailing you coupons for free. You also get free coupon inserts periodically throughout the year in your newspaper. You can also price match. This means that if you see an item on sale in another store's flyer some markets will match or beat the price that is being advertised with their competitor. So instead of wasting gas driving from store to store for sales on different products you just need to shop at one store. Just make sure the flyer's date is current. Never shop when you are hungry. You will grab everything that looks good on the shelves. Instead you should shop with a list. Another way I save money is by eating more vegetarian meals. Meat can be very pricy. I saved about 20% off my grocery bill by just implementing these simple ideas. I saved 2.5% of my budget.

Transportation

When purchasing a car make sure you are buying one you can afford. The best way to buy a car is to pay for it in cash otherwise you will have to lease or finance it. Buy a cheaper, used and more fuel efficient car compared to an expensive new gas guzzling one. You should always shop around and comparison shop before buying. If your car is just eating away at your money consider living in a city where public transportation is available. If you are one to use taxis consider reducing your expense by using the subway or bus to get to where you need to go. If you are a student or an adult with less income or a senior the government will let you purchase bus passes at a discount. By cutting my transportation I saved 59% of my transportation budget which is 7% of my overall budget.

Clothes

Buying used clothes that are in good condition from places such as Goodwill or Value Village (Savers) will save you hundreds of dollars. You might even find brand name items sold considerably less than in a store. Instead of going to the cleaners. Consider washing and ironing your clothes yourself. When buying clothes shop out of season. Ask the sales clerk if they can tell you when items go on sale and mark down their yearly sales cycle on a calendar. By implementing these actions I saved 10% of my expenses.

Entertainment

Instead of going out to the movies with your friends suggest staying in. You can borrow movies and books from your local library. Another option is getting a Netflix subscription. Be aware of your internet usage as watching movies can affect your gigabytes. If you do go to the movies go on cheap days like Monday's or Tuesdays. You can also look for discounted tickets online or some employers offer movie passes as bonuses.

Auto/Home Insurance

If you completed a driver's education program and you are a new driver you can save. Otherwise you can get discounts through your college with some insurance companies if you are a student or alumni.

Textbooks

If you are a student in College or University think about buying your textbooks used either online or through your college book store. You could also rent a textbook or view its electronic version online.

Fitness Classes

Instead of getting a membership at a gym why not go to your local community centers. They offer gym memberships and fitness classes at a discount. You can get special prices if you are a student or senior. There are also free classes available. I personally go to my local community center which offers free yoga classes on Wednesdays. You just need to bring your own yoga mat. I also go swimming at my community center which offers a membership at a discount compared to regular gyms. I saved 3% of my expenses.

Water

You can cut your water bill significantly by simply using water on off peak bill times. This would be after 7pm during the week days and all day on the weekends. I take my showers at night instead of in the morning. I also was my clothes in the evening to save money. You can also save money by taking showers instead of baths. But you should time how long you are showering for and aim for 5-10 minutes. Anything more than that is wasting water. I also save by washing small loads of dishes by hand and washing larger loads in the dish washer. You can also save by lowering your water heater temperature. If you carry out these water saving ideas you will save 15% off your bill which is 5% of my expenses.

Get your notebook and write down 10 expenses that you can cut. Make a detailed plan including the steps you are going to take to cut this expense. Did you know that you are more likely to spend more with credit than with debit and you spend less with cash then with debit? Then you should put away your credit and debit cards and just use cash. Make sure you keep track of your spending in your spending journal. You are also less likely to break a higher denomination bill than a lower. Your mind sees the lower bill as petty cash and with the higher amount it makes it harder to break. Instead of having fives or tens in your wallet consider having twenties, fifties or hundreds. With all the change that you get back from your purchases you should collect it in a jar and use the money you saved to pay off a bill.

So now what? So far you have added up your debt, expenses and income. With that information you have created a monthly budget. You have worked hard on generating more income and found ways of cutting your expenses. So what's next? Well after you have paid off all your debt or are consistently paying your bills and are seeing extra money available to you then you should consider saving. Both how to save and grow your savings will be taught to you in the next two chapters.

Step 7 (week 10): Pay yourself First

Since I was able to not only pay off my debt each month by cutting my expenses but with my extra income I was also able to start saving. I automatically set up transfers into a savings account. By paying yourself first and saving you are setting aside money for emergencies and to build a nest egg.

CHAPTER 7

Savings

How good a saver are you? (Check which apply)

- Do you set goals and plan what you are saving for
- I practice the pay yourself first method
- I have a savings account which is either tax free or earning the most interest compared to other accounts
- I wait a week/month before buying something to make sure I really need it
- Seeing the money in my account rise gives me a thrill
- I grow my savings by investing
- If you earn tips or a bonus from work it goes straight to your savings
- I know exactly how much money I have in my bank accounts
- I have 3-6 months' worth of cash saved for emergencies such as losing a job
- I make saving for retirement my priority

If you got ten out of ten then you are a smart money saver. If you get less than ten but five or more that means you are on your way but you need to make a bit more effort in order to see your money flourish. If you got less than five then you definitely need to read this chapter. Take your binder and make these goal your priority. Jot down ways you can improve your savings. Set dates for your goals and get motivated. You will reach them.

Planned Savings

Setting goals is a great way to plan how you will use your money. This is called planned savings or planned spending depending on the way you want to look at it. Take your notebook and write down a list of things you would like to save for. This may be a vacation, a car or a new television. For example my goal is to save for a vacation to Cuba. Now write down the step you will take in order to achieve this goal. "I will achieve this goal by contributing $50 every paycheck into a savings account". Write down barriers that are keeping you from reaching this goal and explain how you will overcome them. "A barrier to achieving this goal is if I don't have that $50 available to deposit into my savings because I needed to use the money for an emergency. To overcome this barrier I will take extra money I set aside in my tips jar from work as well as sell crafts at a Christmas bazaar to make extra money." Set a date in which you will have saved enough money to reach this goal. "I will reach this goal by May of next year. This is enough time to pay off my trip which I will take in July of next year." You might even get a savings account specifically for this goal. If your goal is short term meaning in a few months. You will have to be able to access your money fairly easy therefore I do not recommend tying it up in stocks. Something simple like a tax-free saving account or esavings account would be perfect for you. Speak with a representative at your bank and tell them your goals. They will help you to choose which investment will be best for your savings goal.

Pay Yourself First

You should practice the pay yourself first method. This means that as soon as your work pay is deposited in your account you should transfer a specific amount every week, biweekly or every month into a savings account. This should be an amount that you can afford to save based on the amount of money you need to use to pay off your bills. This money now insures that you have a means of creating a nest egg for your future. Instead of seeing it as just savings you should see it as something you have to do. By putting the money in a savings account you are allowing it to grow and earn interest. The same time it is out of your checking account so you are less likely to spend it. Make a note to go online and set up an automatic payment from your checking to savings or make an appointment with your bank to assist you with this process.

Savings Accounts

You should always make sure that the bank account you have is earning you the most interest or gives you the best services you can get. Do your research and go online and see what banks are offering. Don't be afraid to call your local financial institutions and speak with a representative if you have any questions regarding their services or concerns about any issues that arise associated with your accounts.

Postponing Purchases

By waiting a week or a month after you've seen something you wanted to buy in a store, you allow yourself the opportunity to really think about your purchase and whether or not you really need it. Could have you used that item this month? Since it's been a month since you've seen the item do you still want it as much as you did when you first saw it. Could the money spent on the item be used differently such as paying a bill or saving for retirement? Write down in your notebook what it is you want to buy and answer the above questions answering why it is you should buy this item. You can do this by writing, "I would really like to buy a new computer but I already have a good one at home to use and I don't need to be spending more money." Another scenario is, "I really need a new printer. The one I currently have is broken and cannot be repaired. I should look for sales on printers because I need one to print out my essays for school."

Stay Motivated

Get addicted to seeing your money rise. Write down how having more wealth can benefit your life. On a small card, jot down the reasons why you are working on saving more and spending less. Now put this in your wallet next to your debit and credit cards. It may be so you can own a home or buy a car. If your family motivates you put a picture of your kids in your wallet. Let their future be the reason why you need to save your money.

Investing

An investment is a certain amount of money that you give into a product such as a stock or bond or in a bank account in hopes that you will earn more for use for a future date. For example you might be putting money into an account and earn interest on it for you to go on a trip to Hawaii two years from now. For further information about savings and investing see chapter 8. Investing is a great way to grow your money but before you invest you need to get educated.

Extra Money

Any extra or unexpected money that you acquire should be first put towards your debt. If you are out of debt and are financially stable a sound choice would be to put that money into savings and not spend it on things you don't need. Take your binder and make a list of items that you wasted your money on and the amount. Now take that amount and add all your purchases up and compare it to something you could have saved for. This may be something you really need like a new lap top for school. If you buy a magazine at $7, every week it adds up to $364. If you eat out twice every week at $10 per meal that's $1040 at the end of the year. You could have bought yourself a really nice lap top for $1404 if you cut out those two expenses each week.

Be Aware of Your Money

You should always know how much money you have in all of your accounts and investments. Set a date each week to go through your accounts, and pay bills. As you go through your statements pay attention to all the money you have. You should know how much you owe and how much you are worth. Making appointments and keeping an up to date record of your financial situation allows you to recognize problems before they arise and fix them. If you didn't look at your bank account you wouldn't notice if the bank accidentally over charged you for their services. If an issue such as this arises then you can contact your financial institution and bring it to their attention so they can correct the error and reimburse you the amount they deducted. Being aware of your money means being aware of problems associated with it.

Emergency fund

We all know those times in life when problems keep arising. You might be out of work for a month or your tire just blew out and you need a new one. This is where the emergency fund comes in. If you have a relatively steady job and reliable source of income then you might need to only save 3 months' worth of money to get you by. If you are an entrepreneur or freelancer and you go months without work then you might need to save up enough money to support yourself for 6 months to a year. Don't forget to include the cost of paying your mortgage each month, putting food on your table and consider extra savings for emergency situations such as paying to fix a leaky roof. Take your binder and use your monthly budget to help you to figure out how much money you should be saving for an emergency. With a financial advisor at your selected financial institution discuss which avenue is the best to hold your emergency savings.

Education Savings

If you are thinking about going to school or have a child that will attend university or college in the future you should consider saving for their education. The Canadian government gives money to parents each year under the child tax benefit. You can use this money and put it into a registered education savings plan. With every deposit you make the government matches a certain percentage. This means that you will not only earn interest but have extra money from the government earning you money too. Each year you should keep contributing your child's tax benefit. Its free money and what better way to use this money than to invest in your child's future.

Home Savings

The cost and maintenance of a home is a huge consideration as to whether or not you should purchase a home as oppose to renting. Before considering buying a home make sure your debt is paid off. You might need to sell your car and be a one car family. You always need to save for a down payment and this is based on the amount of home you are wanting to buy. The amount of down payment you have will also affect how much of a mortgage is available to you. There are several tools like mortgage payment calculators which are available on the internet. You also need to think about the cost of house taxes and extra added bills which you may not have paid when you were renting like hydro. You might have to pay condo fees which are just like having an extra mortgage payment per month. If this is one of your goals then you should be speaking to a financial advisor, and any other professionals associated with home ownership.

Retirement Savings

Everybody knows about the RRSP. How every year, you are allowed to make a contribution that is 18 % of your income which is not taxed. The money you have in your account ideally will not be taxed until it is withdrawn when you are retired. Free money that not everyone thinks about is the amount of money that their company pension plan can give them. Some plans match dollar per dollar every contribution you make. If you have any benefits or pension plan with your company you should find out and make use of it. There are also outside companies that you can approach that allow you to make payments towards a pension which they give you when you have retired. You can look online for these companies. You might also use the money from your house and sell it and retire off of it. Another way to grow your retirement money is to invest in stocks or mutual funds. If you have this goal in mind then speak with a financial advisor. You should also go online and your local library to educate yourself more about investing in your retirement future.

Tax Refund

One great way is to use your tax refund to buy RRSPs or deposit in your TSFA. Each year you get money back you can use it to plan for retirement or any other savings. Your money will grow and its money you don't even think about. To ensure that you will get a refund look at your paycheck and see how much the government deducts. If they aren't taking enough taxes off your earnings then you will have to pay more taxes at the end of the year. This becomes a problem when you haven't saved enough money to pay back the taxes owed. You can fill out a form and request that the accounting administrator at your work deduct more taxes off your pay.

So now you have no excuse but to start saving. You have learned how to plan your expenses and save for the future. You have seen how important it is to pay yourself first and learned about savings accounts. You have practiced self-discipline and postponed purchases as well as stayed motivated by seeing your savings rise. You have learned about investing and what you should do with the extra money you get. You have seen the importance of being aware of your money and have been taught to identify problems and correct them. You have created an emergency fund and started saving for an education, a home or retirement. Now off to the next chapter to flourish your savings.

Step 8 (week 11 & 12): Grow your savings

In a few months my savings grew but I was a little greedy and I researched ways I could make my money work for me and growing it faster. This meant I could have larger amounts of money in the future to use for my goals such as owning a home, and retiring.

CHAPTER 8

How to grow your savings

Now that you have gained insight as to what you're saving for it is important to inform yourself on how to make your money work for you. This is done through investing. By investing sooner than later you give your money time to grow. This means you should start young. If you have children then it is your responsibility to teach them about savings and help them to open up their own savings account. Show them how investing works by reviewing how much interest their money earns monthly. Even if you are young as 18 and don't have much money you can start investing. Some financial institutions allow you to invest as low as $500 into mutual funds or GICs. That little amount of money can grow substantially. Different types of investments include a TFSA, Esavings account, GICs, mutual funds, stocks and bonds. No one option is better than the other. It all depends on your level of risk tolerance and how many years you have to grow your investment.

What Type of Investor are you?

	Agree	Neutral	Disagree
I am young			
I have good investment knowledge			

I enjoy roller coasters			
New opportunities and ventures excite me			
I am looking to invest for several years			
Losing a little money doesn't bother me			
I'm looking to diversify my investments			
I have a good relationship with my financial advisor			
People think of me as someone who lives on the edge			

If you checked off agree for most of the questions then you are a risk taker. You should invest in stocks. If you are young it means you have more years to ride through the falls of an investment. You are also willing to take the risk of losing your investment just for the chance of receiving a large gain. If you checked of neutral then you are a moderate investor. A good option for you are mutual funds. This will allow you to grow your money with less risk. If you disagreed to most of the statement you are a very cautious person. You might be older and not able to withstand large losses of money because you won't have enough time to gain it back. Investing in a TSFA or GIC is perfect for you.

TSFA (Tax Free Savings Account)

This is an investment created by the government to push people to start saving money. Each year you are allowed to deposit $5,500 into your account. The interest that you earn is not taxed. You are also able to take out your money more quickly than you would another investment. You can use a TSFA to save for just about everything. One person might use it to save for a computer another might use it to save for a new air conditioner.

Whatever you choose to save for make sure you deposit within your limits. For example since you are only allowed to deposit $5500 per year and you deposit $2500 in February then in July you take out that $2500 to repair your roof. This does not mean you can redeposit the whole $5000. You can only contribute $3000 into your account for that year. For more information on the rules of the TSFA go to your financial intuition's website.

Esavings

Electronic savings account. This means that you wouldn't go to a teller. You would be using online banking to manage your account. Many banks offer this type of savings account because it yields greater interest for the client. Meaning with all the fees associated with managing paper work, the banks save money and pass their savings to you. This option is for someone who wants to have more control over how they manage their money. They must also be familiar with computers. This account is taxed. You must consider the amount of interest you earn and how much it's taxed compared to less interest and no tax in a TSFA. You can use this account to save for vacations or use it to store your emergency fund.

GIC (Guaranteed Investment Certificate)

A Guaranteed Investment Certificate (GIC) is a type of investment that is considered safe. Why? Because it guarantees that you will get the whole investment you put in plus the agreed upon interest. You earn interest that is based on how long you have it for. Your investment is less liquid meaning that in an emergency you will not be able to take out your money and use it. It will be tied up for a few months or years. Don't use it as an emergency fund instead you can use it for future goals such as saving money for a down payment on a house.

Mutual Fund

It is where a professional who is managing a portfolio of stocks, bonds and other investments on behalf of individual investors. Each investor owns a share of the investment portfolio. By diversifying and having a portfolio which contains a wide arrange of investments it ensure that you don't put all your eggs in one basket. This means you are not investing in just one thing. If one investment does poorly their will likely be another that is doing well which enables you to minimize the loss of money. By having a mutual fund it enables you to purchase a share at a lower cost where all the investor's cash are combined to purchase a variety of stocks or bonds. The down side is that there may be fees associated with this investment like sales charges or management fees. You would use a mutual fund for someone who is a moderate type of investor and saving for a long-term goal such as Retirement.

Stock

By purchasing a stock you are investing in a share of the company. This means that you own a certain percentage of a company depending on how many stocks are sold. This type of investment are for risk takers. Holding a share of a company means that you will see rises and falls depending on if the company is making a profit or losing money. Investing in a business is a big decision and can be very difficult. There are many new business offering new products which you don't have much financial history therefore you don't really know how well their product will do on the market. You are essentially taking a chance. A good rule is to invest an amount of money that you would be comfortable losing. Stocks are considered volatile. This is a term used to describe the fact that it is unpredictable.

Bonds

A bond is a debt that a business incurs by borrowing money from a large group of people. Unlike a stock where you own a portion of the business, you don't own the company you are simply lending them money in hopes that they pay you back with interest. Again lending money through a bond is like a stock in a sense being that you don't know how well the business will do and there is no guarantee that you will get your money back if the business does poorly and goes bankrupt.

Canada Savings Bond

This is a very safe type of bond. This is because it is insured by the government which means unlike regular bonds where you might not get your money back, with this bond you will. They are only available at certain times throughout the year. But you can invest a minimum of $100 which is locked in for 90 days.

The more different ways of investing the more diversified your financial portfolio. The less risk of loss. Whichever investment options you choose is up to you and should be based on your needs as well as how well you can access your money. If you need to access your money fast then a TSFA, or Esavings account is great for you. If you are into growing your funds more but want less risk then a GIC or mutual fund is right for you. Or if you want to diversify your financial portfolio, you can add bonds or stocks. Don't lend money for which you can't afford to lose. People have lost money with stocks and bonds but they have also gained a greater amount of money than they would with other investments. Before investing in stocks or bonds you should ensure that you have a financial advisor that you trust as well as you should research the company you are investing in. There are many venues for you to choose to grow your money. If you do your research and work with a trusted financial institution you'll have no problem saving your nest egg now and hatching it in the future into a golden goose.

CHAPTER 9

On-Going Financial Maintenance

The work doesn't stop here. Now that you have completed the 8 steps in just three months, you shouldn't stop. In order for you to be out of debt for life is by continually working with your money. I found that I needed to continue my work to keep from going back into debt and to continue to save for my goals. There is on-going maintenance that needs to be done every day, week, month and year. Here's what you need to do:

Every day

- Dream and fantasize about what you want to achieve in your life and how it would feel to own a home, get educated and get a good job or retire with enough money to support yourself.
- Use your spending journal and record every transaction you make. Have two categories one for your debit card and one for your credit card. You should know your balances.
- Collect your tips or bonuses and use it to pay off a debt or save for the future.
- Write in a journal what made you happy that day. Was it seeing a smile on your child's face while she was playing

an organized sport which you paid for with money you saved?

Every Week

- You will have to pay your bills and make sure you pay them on time and in advance to make sure the transaction goes through in your bank. Keep due dates on a calendar.
- Practice being aware of your money by going through statements and purchases you made that week. Make sure that everything is accounted for and there are no mistakes.
- Practice Paying yourself first and make sure every time you get paid you are putting away money to save for your financial goal
- Post pone purchases that you feel you think you would make on impulse. Instead plan what you want to buy and where your money is going. Consider if you need it or if you could do without it.

Every Month

- Use your spending journal to help you add up your expenses. Use that information to fill in your budget. See if you are over or under and adjust your spending accordingly.
- Cut your expenses further and see what you can do without that month. To give you extra money for emergencies.
- Write down in your journal new ways of saving or making money that you can do next month.
- Set monthly goals and make sure you stay on target. A goal could be find a way to save $100 in the beginning of the month so you could use it to plan your child's birthday party at the end of the month.

Every Year

- Get your credit score. Is it low or high? Think of ways on why it improved or how you can improve it further.
- Set up a date to review your investments with your financial planner. Discuss with them how your investments did and how you can better grow your money.
- Set yearly financial goals. Such as vacations and plan on how you can reach it throughout the year.
- Go to your annual physical exam with your doctor and make sure you are healthy. How your health is will affect your ability on qualifying for life insurance which effects your family's financial well-being.

Being financially independent, debt free, and happy depends on how much responsibility you take with your money. There is no quick fix just hard work. If you keep on with your daily, weekly, month, and yearly responsibilities, you will definitely reach your long-term goals such as retirement.

CONCLUSION

Congratulations! You've don't it! You've worked hard these twelve weeks and changed your financial future. You were like a Picasso painting, you went from having a future that was unclear and consisting of fear by not knowing how you could afford to live because of your debt. Feeling like there is no way out. Now your future is like a Monet painting full of landscapes, beautiful colors and possibilities. Like an artist who controls every spec of color, he holds his brush and creates every movement and swirl. You too can paint your own financial future by controlling you're spending and planning the future you want to create. You can achieve your goals and reach high to the sky and attain your dreams. It just takes some work, a little planning and a lot of dreaming. Now that you are about to embark into a future full of happiness and possibilities I say to you, paint on!